The St. Lawrence

River Route to the Great Lakes

By Lynn Peppas

CRABTREE
Publishing Company
www.crabtreebooks.com

Crabtree Publishing Company

www.crabtreebooks.com

Author: Lynn Peppas
Editor: Barbara Bakowski
Designer: Tammy West, Westgraphix LLC
Photo Researcher: Edward A. Thomas
Map Illustrator: Stefan Chabluk
Indexer: Nila Glikin
Project Coordinator: Kathy Middleton
Crabtree Editor: Adrianna Morganelli
Proofreader: Reagan Miller
Production Coordinator: Kenneth Wright
Prepress Technician: Kenneth Wright

Series Consultant: Michael E. Ritter, Ph.D., Professor
of Geography, University of Wisconsin—Stevens Point

Developed for Crabtree Publishing Company by RJF
Publishing LLC (www.RJFpublishing.com)

Photo Credits:
Cover, 6, 7, 9, 19: iStockphoto;
4: ESCUDERO Patrick/Hernis/Photolibrary
10: Gary Cralle/Photographer's Choice/Getty Images
13: Norbert Rosing/Oxford Scientific/Photolibrary
14: Bruno Perousse/age fotostock/Photolibrary
16 (top): Stock Montage/Getty Images
16 (bottom): © Jeff Greenberg/Alamy
18: © North Wind/North Wind Picture Archives
20: © North Wind Picture Archives/Alamy
22: National Geographic/Getty Images
23: Rolf Hicker/All Canada Photos/Getty Images
24: © Robert Estall photo agency/Alamy
27: AP Images
25: © Bert Hoferichter/Alamy

Cover: An oil ship traveling the St. Lawrence River passes
Quebec City.

Library and Archives Canada Cataloguing in Publication

Peppas, Lynn
    The St. Lawrence : river route to the Great Lakes / Lynn Peppas.

(Rivers around the world)
Includes index.
ISBN 978-0-7787-7447-1 (bound).--ISBN 978-0-7787-7470-9 (pbk.)

    1. Saint Lawrence River--Juvenile literature. 2. Saint Lawrence
River
Valley--Juvenile literature. I. Title. II. Series: Rivers around the
world

FC2756.P46 2010   j971.4   C2009-906245-3

Library of Congress Cataloging-in-Publication Data

Peppas, Lynn.
    The St. Lawrence : river route to the Great Lakes / by Lynn Peppas.
        p. cm. -- (Rivers around the world)
    Includes index.
    ISBN 978-0-7787-7470-9 (pbk. : alk. paper) -- ISBN 978-0-7787-7447-1
(reinforced library binding : alk. paper)
    1. Saint Lawrence River--Juvenile literature. 2. Saint Lawrence
River Valley--Juvenile literature. I. Title. II. Series.

F1050.P47 2009
971.4--dc22

                                                     2009042410

Crabtree Publishing Company
www.crabtreebooks.com   1-800-387-7650

Printed in the U.S.A./122009/BG20091103

Published in Canada
Crabtree Publishing
616 Welland Ave.
St. Catharines, ON
L2M 5V6

Published in the United States
Crabtree Publishing
PMB 59051
350 Fifth Avenue, 59th Floor
New York, New York 10118

Published in the UnitedKingdom
Crabtree Publishing
Maritime House
Basin Road North, Hove
BN41 1WR

Published in Australia
Crabtree Publishing
386 Mt. Alexander Rd.
Ascot Vale (Melbourne)
VIC 3032

CONTENTS

Words that are defined in the glossary are in **bold** type
the first time they appear in the text.

CHAPTER 1

An Important Waterway

The St. Lawrence River is neither the largest nor the longest river in the world—or even in Canada. Still, its importance in shaping North America both historically and economically makes it one of the greatest rivers on the continent.

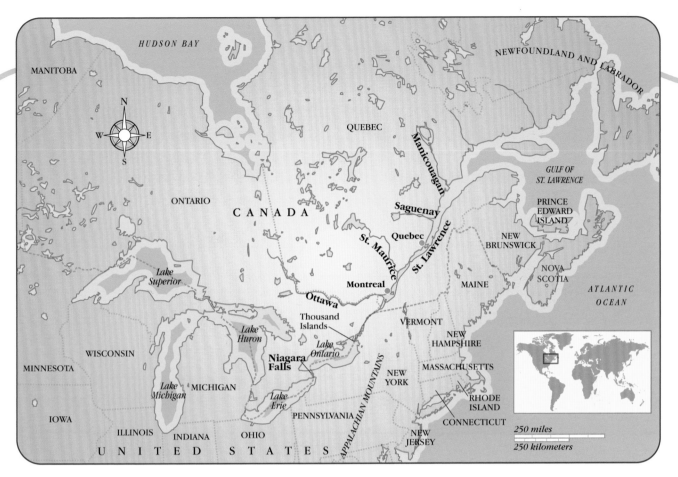

The St. Lawrence River flows east from Lake Ontario to the Gulf of St. Lawrence, where it empties into the Atlantic Ocean.

The St. Lawrence River has long attracted people to its tree-lined shores. Thousands of years ago, **indigenous**, or native, people used the river as a means of transportation. They settled along the St. Lawrence River's shores and used the area's natural resources. The river supplied fresh drinking water, food such as fish and other animals that lived along the river, and young trees for building shelters.

LEFT: Visible from the restored port of Old Montreal in Quebec, the silver dome of Bonsecours Market was once a landmark for ships entering the harbor.

FAST FACT

The St. Lawrence River is the 19th-longest river in the world. It is the third-longest river in Canada.

5

Great River, Great Lakes

The five large lakes in central North America are named the Great Lakes for good reason. These five freshwater lakes—Superior, Huron, Michigan, Erie, and Ontario—hold about one-fifth of Earth's fresh surface water. Lake Superior contains the largest volume of water, equal to all the other Great Lakes combined. The lakes are connected to one another by narrow channels. Through the channels, water drains toward Lake Ontario, located farthest east, and into the St. Lawrence River, which flows northeast into the Atlantic Ocean. The Niagara River, which connects Lake Erie to Lake Ontario, contains the world-famous Niagara Falls. At the falls, the water spills almost 170 feet (50 meters) from wide cliffs on both the U.S. and Canadian shores.

More than 3,000 tons (2,720 metric tons) of water flows over Niagara Falls every second.

In the 1500s, European explorers discovered that the St. Lawrence River was a pathway into North America. Although the river was not the route to Asia they had hoped to find, many Europeans found the area to be a rich treasure chest of natural resources. They set up settlements and trading posts, where they traded European goods such as knives for animal furs brought in by indigenous people. Eventually, large cities such as Montreal and Quebec City, both in the Canadian province of Quebec, grew up along the river.

A Modern View

Today, the St. Lawrence River is important for a number of reasons. Sections of the river act as a border between Canada and the United States, providing both nations with a renewable energy source and a shipping route. The St. Lawrence River also carries water from the largest freshwater system of lakes in the world—the Great Lakes.

A great volume of **commodities**, or products, moves on the St. Lawrence River and Seaway through a series of **locks**, **canals**, and waterways built by

During the winter months, a thick crust of ice covers the St. Lawrence River. Icebreakers maintain an open channel for shipping.

NOTABLE QUOTE

"On both sides of the [St. Lawrence] River there are good and fair grounds, full of as fair and mighty trees as any be in the world.... There are a great store of Oaks, the most excellent that ever I saw in my life.... Besides this there are fairer Maples, Cedars, Beeches, and other trees than grown in France."

—French explorer Jacques Cartier, in records of his third voyage to North America, May 1541

the governments of Canada and the United States. The canals and locks of the St. Lawrence Seaway enable ships to travel from the Atlantic Ocean more than 2,300 miles (3,700 kilometers) into the interior of North America.

Powerful Flow

At power stations along the St. Lawrence River, the river's enormous amounts of moving water are used to produce electricity. **Hydroelectricity** generated by the St. Lawrence River supplies power to many people in Canada and the United States.

Protecting the River

The St. Lawrence River's abundant power and its accessibility as a transportation route made its shores an ideal location for factories, such as

steel, cement, food processing, and other manufacturing plants. Industrial development along the St. Lawrence River negatively affected the river's **ecology**. The release of chemicals from factories polluted the waters. By the 1970s, the St. Lawrence River was one of the most polluted large rivers in the world. Dams, built to create **reservoirs** for hydroelectric plants, changed the current in the river, affecting animal **habitats** and disturbing the **migration** of certain fish species.

Over the past few decades, the U.S. and Canadian governments have worked to control pollution and protect the river's ecology. Today, the St. Lawrence River is one of the cleanest rivers in the world. Many organizations now protect wildlife species and their habitats, too.

Many Things to Many People

People are still drawn to the shores of the St. Lawrence River by some of the same benefits that formerly attracted indigenous people and early European explorers and settlers. These features include **economic** opportunities and a wealth of natural resources and beauty. Today, millions of people live along the St. Lawrence River. Many visitors from around the world still explore the river, enjoying its untouched natural beauty and its cities filled with culture and history. From the Thousand Islands, near Lake Ontario, to Quebec City, the power and natural beauty of the river have inspired writers and artists.

FAST FACT

More than 35 million people live in the Great Lakes-St. Lawrence River basin.

The Thousand Islands region is actually made up of about 1,800 islands, from small, rocky formations to much larger landmasses.

CHAPTER 2
Along the St. Lawrence River

From the eastern tip of Lake Ontario to the Gulf of St. Lawrence, the St. Lawrence River flows through different landscapes—from small rocky islands to farm fields, lush forests, and rocky beaches—as it flows eastward toward its **mouth** at the Atlantic Ocean. The river flows through two Canadian provinces and borders one U.S. state, New York, before coming to the Gulf of St. Lawrence, where it then makes its way into the Atlantic Ocean. In some places, the course broadens into calm **fluvial** lakes, such as Lakes Saint-François, Saint-Louis, and Saint-Pierre. Elsewhere, the river narrows into fast-moving rapids, such as the Lachine Rapids near Montreal.

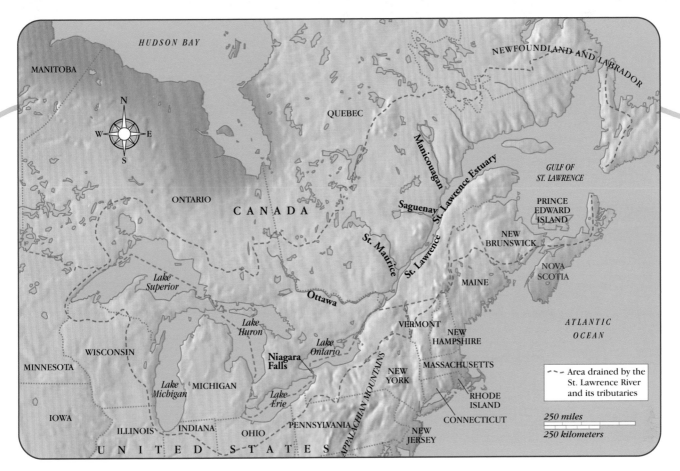

The St. Lawrence River system drains 502,000 square miles (1.3 million square km) of land.

Ancient River

The Saint Lawrence River began forming thousands of years ago, during the last ice age. A huge **glacier** covered the region. As the glacier moved over the surface of North America, it gouged out areas of the landscape and deposited rock and soil in other areas. Mountains, valleys, and lakebeds formed in the process. The glacier began to melt about 12,000 years ago, and water began filling the Great Lakes. Water also flooded much of the region through

LEFT: A lighthouse on the red cliffs of île du Havre-Aubert overlooks the Gulf of St. Lawrence.

FAST FACT

About 350 million years ago, a huge meteorite slammed into Earth, leaving a bowl-shaped depression in present-day Quebec. The Charlevoix **crater**, which is 34 miles (55 km) wide, is partly covered by the St. Lawrence River.

11

which the St. Lawrence River now flows, creating a body of water scientists call the Champlain Sea. Over thousands of years, the land beneath the sea shifted upward, and the water drained northeastward into the Atlantic Ocean. Eventually, by about 6,500 to 6,000 years ago, just the present channel of the St. Lawrence River remained as a body of water.

Going With the Flow

The St. Lawrence River starts off with a powerful surge of water gathered from the Great Lakes. The river's 744-mile (1,190-km) course begins at the eastern end of Lake Ontario. There the river flows through the Thousand Islands, a popular tourist area. These rocky islands are at the southernmost tip of the geographic region known as the Canadian Shield.

The stretch of the river from Lake Ontario to the city of Cornwall, Ontario, is an international boundary between Canada and the United States. East of Cornwall, the river flows through only Canada for the rest of its course. In eastern Canada the river flows through a geographic region called the St. Lawrence Lowlands. This area's rich soil was deposited thousands of years ago by the glacier that scraped across this part of North America.

To the south of the river is the Appalachian geographic region. The Appalachian Mountains are one of the oldest mountain ranges on Earth. This region also supports agriculture. Farmers grow fruits, vegetables, grains, and food crops for livestock.

The St. Lawrence River widens into a huge **estuary**. There the freshwater mixes with saltwater from the ocean. At the mouth of the St. Lawrence, the river empties into the Atlantic Ocean.

Down the Drain

The St. Lawrence River system's **drainage basin**, including the Great

A Mingling of Waters

About 335 miles (540 km) long and up to 90 miles (145 km) wide at its eastern end, the St. Lawrence estuary is one of the largest in the world. It begins just north of Lake St.-Pierre, near the city of Trois-Rivières, in Quebec, Canada. There the estuary widens to about three miles (five km) from shore to shore. Twice a day, the freshwater levels rise and fall with the tides of the Atlantic Ocean. Beyond a large island called Île d'Orleans, the estuary widens to more than nine miles (15 km), and the freshwater of the river mixes with the saltwater from the Atlantic Ocean.

Lakes system, is the world's 13th-largest river basin. A river's drainage basin is the land drained by the river and its **tributaries**. A river's **drainage pattern** is the arrangement of the main stream and its tributaries. The St. Lawrence River's tributaries include the Ottawa River, the Manicouagan River, the Saint Maurice River, and the Saguenay River. Both **trellis** and **dendritic** drainage patterns occur in the St. Lawrence drainage basin. A trellis pattern looks like crossed strips. A dendritic pattern looks like the branches of a tree.

Plant and Animal Life

The variety of geographic regions in the St. Lawrence River basin results in a diversity of plants and animals. Evergreen forests of pine, cedar, and hemlock cover much of the land north of the St. Lawrence River. To the south of the river are maple, oak, and birch trees. Plants that grow well in salty soil, such as the beach groundsel and the sea milkwort, live in the estuary.

Harbor seals make their homes in the St. Lawrence estuary year round. Harp seals live in the river in winter and spring, when the females give birth to pups. More than 100 freshwater fish species, including yellow perch, salmon, trout, American eel, catfish, and sunfish, also live in the river.

Whales and walruses were once plentiful in the St. Lawrence estuary but were almost hunted to **extinction** in the 1700s and 1800s. Whales were hunted for their hides and for oil, which was used in lamps and candle wax. Walruses were hunted for their ivory tusks, leather skins, and oil. Today, only beluga whales and porpoises remain.

Laws protect the approximately 1,000 beluga whales that currently live in the St. Lawrence estuary.

CHAPTER 3

Settling the St. Lawrence

The people and settlements along the shores of the St. Lawrence River are diverse. The rich soil of the St. Lawrence Lowlands makes the region ideal for growing crops. Much of this land today is rural, with large, open fields and small populations. Most of the people in the region live in bustling cities, such as Montreal, with a population of almost two million people. Quebec City—the oldest city along the river—is home to almost 700,000 people.

In 1763, France lost almost all of its possessions in eastern North America to Great Britain, which then controlled the entire area in green on the map at right. The dark green area contained the colonies ruled directly by the British government.

First Nations

Since about 10,000 years ago, groups of indigenous people have lived in eastern Canada. First the Algonquin and later the Iroquois settled in the St. Lawrence region. The Algonquin people lived north of the river. The Iroquois people settled to the south. Native people living near the river used it for transportation, for fishing, and as a source of freshwater. They also hunted deer, fish, moose, and rabbits. They gathered berries and grew corn, squash, and beans.

European Explorers

During the 1500s, European explorers arrived at the St. Lawrence River. They were looking for a sea route to Asia, where they hoped to trade their goods for valuable spices. In 1497, the Italian explorer John Cabot had claimed for

LEFT: The Château Frontenac, a castle-like hotel, is the most prominent feature of the Quebec City skyline and is a symbol of the city.

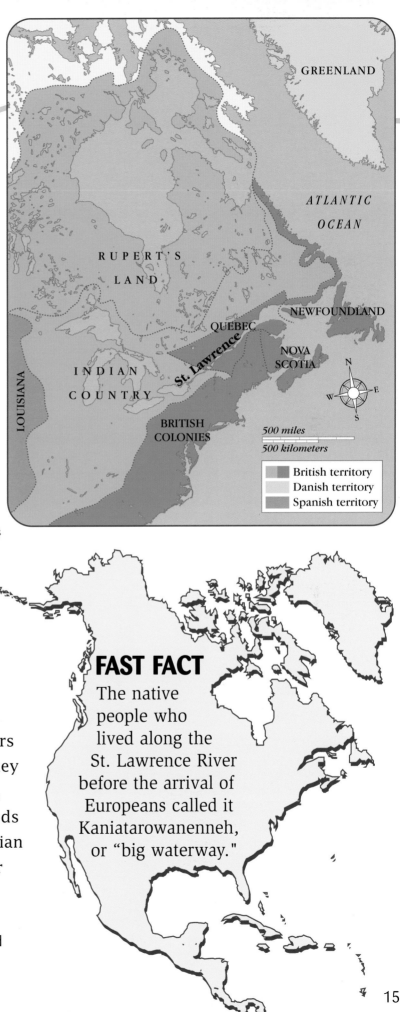

GREENLAND

ATLANTIC OCEAN

RUPERT'S LAND

NEWFOUNDLAND

QUEBEC

NOVA SCOTIA

INDIAN COUNTRY

St. Lawrence

LOUISIANA

BRITISH COLONIES

N W E S

500 miles
500 kilometers

British territory
Danish territory
Spanish territory

FAST FACT
The native people who lived along the St. Lawrence River before the arrival of Europeans called it Kaniatarowanenneh, or "big waterway."

15

Cartier's Voyages

French explorer Jacques Cartier (1491–1557) was the first known European to sail inland along the St. Lawrence River. The king of France financed Cartier's first voyage in hopes the explorer would discover gold and an ocean passage to Asia. During Cartier's second voyage, most of his sailors died of scurvy, a disease caused by not eating enough fruits and vegetables containing vitamin C. Cartier returned to France, kidnapping and taking with him a chief of the Algonquin nation, his two sons, and two others. All five died of disease before Cartier returned to Canada on a third voyage, in 1541.

French navigator and explorer Jacques Cartier

Street signs in French in Montreal, Quebec, reflect the region's colonial history.

England the area now called Newfoundland. Other explorers soon followed, looking for a passage to Asia. In 1534, Jacques Cartier from France sailed into the Gulf of St. Lawrence but turned back before continuing on to the St. Lawrence River. In 1535, he returned and sailed up the river into central Canada. Cartier claimed the area for his homeland of France.

Furs and Fish

Although other Europeans tried to start colonies along the St. Lawrence River, French explorer Samuel de Champlain first succeeded in 1608. Earlier efforts had failed because of harsh winter conditions, diseases, and lack of food. Champlain succeeded because he had built a relationship with neighboring Algonquin tribes, who taught the European colonists which foods to eat to prevent diseases. Champlain established a fort and trading post at what is now Quebec City. The Europeans traded goods such as knives, blankets, and household items with indigenous people for furs, especially beaver pelts, which were sent to Europe to make fashionable clothing. Basques, people who came from the western Pyrenees and the Bay of Biscay in Spain and France, arrived to fish in the St. Lawrence River and to hunt whales off the Canadian coast.

Story of a Name

On August 10, 1535, during his second voyage to Canada, Jacques Cartier discovered a bay near the mouth of the St. Lawrence River. Cartier and his fellow sailors celebrated this date as the feast day of Saint Lawrence. Saint Lawrence was a Christian who had been put to death for his faith by a Roman ruler on this date in 258. Cartier gave the saint's name to the bay. Eventually, the name St. Lawrence came to be used for the entire river.

War Breaks Out

Champlain **allied** himself with the Algonquin. The French fur traders faced threats from the Iroquois, who were often at war with the Algonquin, and the British, who were beginning to explore Canada and claim the land.

The French controlled the land north of the St. Lawrence River. British settlers began trading furs with the Iroquois, to the south. Because the climate in the south was warmer, those furs were not as thick—or as valuable—as furs from the colder region to the north. The two European nations had a long history of war, and battles broke out between the French and the British in Canada. The Iroquois

FAST FACT

Francophones, or French-speaking people, in Canada call the river Rivière Saint-Laurent.

and the Algonquin had fought each other for many years, too. The conflict reached a climax in 1754, when the French and Indian War broke out in North America. The British were allied with the Iroquois, and the French with the Algonquin. The British won the war in 1763. The Treaty of Paris, a written agreement that ended the war, awarded virtually all French territory in eastern North America to the British. In 1791, the British divided a large part of their territory in eastern Canada into Upper Canada,

This woodcut shows the British capturing Quebec in 1759 during the French and Indian War.

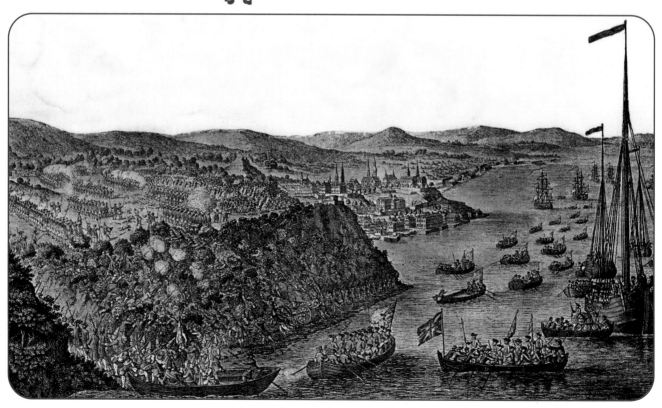

Founded by French settlers on an island in the St. Lawrence River in 1642, Montreal is today the largest city in the province of Quebec and the second-largest city in Canada, after Toronto.

the southern part of modern-day Ontario, and Lower Canada, the southern part of present-day Quebec. Upper Canada had more English settlers and Lower Canada more French residents. Today, the two provinces of Ontario and Quebec still have somewhat distinct cultures.

NOTABLE QUOTE

"It would be very difficult to ascertain the character of this region without spending a winter in it; for, on arriving here in summer, every thing is very agreeable.... There are six months of winter in this country.... During the winter, in the deepest snows, [the Native people] hunt elks and other animals.... When they go hunting, they use a kind of snow-shoe twice as large as those hereabouts, which they attach to the soles of their feet, and walk thus over the snow without sinking in."

—Samuel de Champlain, *Voyages of Samuel de Champlain*, Vol. II

CHAPTER 4

Travel and Commerce

When European explorers first arrived in North America, the landscape looked very different from the way it appears today. Untamed forests and rocky terrain made early exploration by land very difficult. The St. Lawrence River offered explorers who came by ship an easy route into central North America. Although their goal was to find a trade route to Asia, these sailors discovered a wealth of goods that could be reached, and traded, on the St. Lawrence River. Eventually, the French and British set up trading posts and colonies. The region's history is still evident, 500 years later, in the present-day **bilingual** country of Canada.

Native Navigation

Indigenous people were the first to use the St. Lawrence River as a means of travel. The Algonquin used the wood of young birch trees to build lightweight canoes, which they covered with birch bark. These first boats were good for navigating a river that could change from calm waters to churning rapids quite quickly along its course. Canoes could carry large loads and withstand the rigors of river travel, yet they were light enough to be carried over land.

Trade, Fishing, and Logging

For the first 100 years after Europeans arrived in North America, their primary purpose for navigating the St. Lawrence was trade. Settlements were simply trading posts on the river. Native people and French fur trappers relied on the river as an easy transportation route to ship beaver pelts and other furs that were in great demand in Europe. The Basques relied on the river for fish, which they then transported to Spain. Off the Atlantic coast, they hunted walruses and beluga whales for oil, hides (or skin), and meat. Some Basque people eventually stayed year-round and settled in the St. Lawrence River valley.

Europeans discovered another valuable natural resource in North America: lumber. Again, the St. Lawrence River provided a convenient way to move the product. Lumberjacks cut down trees and used horses to drag the logs to the river. There the logs were tied together to form rafts, which were floated downstream. When the rafts reached Montreal or Quebec City, the lumber was loaded onto ships and sent to Europe to be used as building supplies.

Lachine Canal

Until the 1700s, ships could travel inland on the St. Lawrence River only as far as Montreal. The Lachine Rapids prevented them from sailing farther west. Lachine comes from the French name for China. Early French explorers hoped that China lay beyond the impassable rapids.

In the late 1600s, a French monk named François Dollier de Casson planned to dig a canal that would bypass the rapids. But the Iroquois objected to the construction of a canal

LEFT: French fur traders used canoes to travel on the St. Lawrence River.

St. Lawrence Seaway

Eighteenth-century Basque whalers hunting off the shore of Newfoundland

The St. Lawrence Seaway enables large cargo ships to travel between the Atlantic Ocean and ports all along the St. Lawrence River and in the Great Lakes—transporting goods west or east through North America for up to thousands of miles. Construction began in 1954. An effort by the governments of both Canada and the United States, the project took five years to complete.

The St. Lawrence Seaway's system of canals, locks, and dams bypassed or overcame natural obstacles—along the river or between the lakes—that had prevented travel by ocean-going ships. The seaway thus opened up an important commercial shipping route from Europe into central North America. Seven locks were built in the

and in 1689 attacked the French settlers. The canal was put on hold for more than a century. When the Casson Canal, now called the Lachine Canal, was finally completed in 1824, it changed transportation on the St. Lawrence River dramatically and contributed to the growth of Montreal as a major industrial center.

NOTABLE QUOTE

"Men have dreamed and worked for two and a half centuries to make this river navigable, and now at last it is a reality. This waterway…will…exercise a profound influence on the maritime trading nations of the world."

—Queen Elizabeth II of the United Kingdom, at the formal opening of the St. Lawrence Seaway in 1959

What Are Locks?

Locks are like water steps that enable ships to move between areas of different elevations. A ship enters a lock and is enclosed by two watertight gates. If the ship is traveling downstream, water is released through **valves** in the gates until the ship is lowered to the level of the water it is entering. If it is traveling upstream, water is allowed in through valves in the gates to raise the ship.

Montreal–Lake Ontario section of the seaway to lift vessels to 246 feet (75 m) above sea level. The Welland Canal, a waterway link between Lakes Ontario and Erie, was first built in 1829, to bypass Niagara Falls. The present canal was completed in 1932 and deepened as part of the seaway project. Today the canal's eight locks lift ships 326 feet (100 m). Ships now carry large containers filled with iron ore, steel, chemicals, grain, and other goods between the Atlantic and the center of North America.

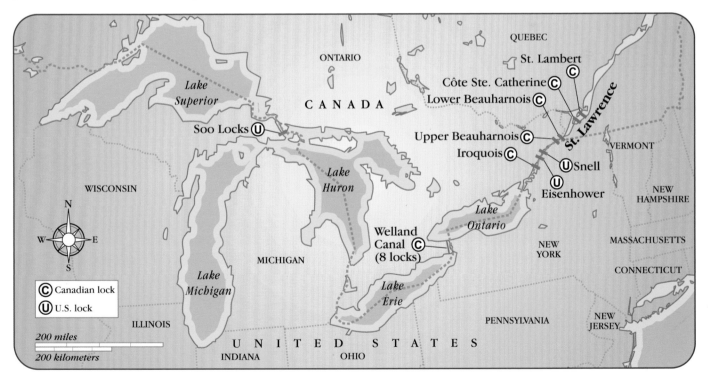

The St. Lawrence Seaway includes 15 locks that enable navigation from Montreal to Lake Erie. To the northwest, the Soo locks at Sault Ste. Marie, Michigan, link the upper Great Lakes and Lake Superior.

CHAPTER 5

The St. Lawrence River Today

The St. Lawrence River remains important to businesses in many North American communities along its shores. Millions of people live within one mile (1.6 km) of the river's shores. Stretches of the river and its rocky cliffs, sandy shores, cityscapes, and canals and locks attract a large number of tourists to the region, especially during the summer.

Tourism and Culture

The Thousand Islands area has been a summer vacation spot since the late 1800s and remains popular with fishers and boaters today. One of the most popular attractions in this area is the historic Boldt Castle on the U.S. side of the St. Lawrence River. The owner, George Boldt, built the castle for his wife, but she died before construction was completed. He abandoned the project, and it remained unfinished until 1977. At that time, the Thousand Islands Bridge Authority repaired and restored Boldt Castle.

The two cities on the river with the largest populations, Quebec City and Montreal, are also two of the oldest cities in Canada. Both have a vibrant French-Canadian culture. Quebec City's annual winter carnival, called Carnaval, is known worldwide for its snow sculpture contest, ice hotels, and sports competitions on the frozen St. Lawrence River.

Boldt Castle is now a popular tourist attraction in the Thousand Islands area.

Hydroelectricity

The St. Lawrence River is also an important source of electric power. Sizable drops in elevation in various sections of the river make it ideal for hydroelectric power production. The river and many of its tributaries have dams and power plants that harness the movement of falling water to turn **turbines** and generate electricity.

The Beauharnois hydroelectric power station was built between 1929 and 1932. It was later expanded to meet the growing demand for electricity. Today, almost 85 percent of the St. Lawrence River's flow passes through the power plant, which is

LEFT: The Robert Moses–Robert H. Saunders Power Dam produces electricity for both Canada and the United States.

Saving the Eels

Hydroelectricity is a clean, renewable source of energy. However, the construction of power plants has had harmful effects on the ecology of the St. Lawrence River. For example, the American eel population has declined. American eels breed in the Sargasso Sea, south of Bermuda and east of the Carolinas in the western Atlantic. The eels swim downstream in the St. Lawrence River as they migrate to their breeding grounds. As river water passes through the power plant, some eels are killed by the action of the spinning turbines that are used to generate electricity. The barriers created by hydro dams also block young eels from migrating back upstream to their freshwater habitat in the upper St. Lawrence River and the Great Lakes. An eel ladder has been installed at the Robert Moses-Robert H. Saunders Power Dam to help migrating eels bypass the dam. The ladder is like a water staircase for fish!

located about 25 miles (40 km) south of Montreal. The facility supplies power to Montreal and other areas in the province of Quebec.

The Robert Moses–Robert H. Saunders hydroelectric generating station was built from 1954 to 1958 as a joint Canadian–U.S. project. The power dam spans the St. Lawrence River from Massena, New York, to Cornwall, Ontario. The dam is the length of ten football fields! With 32 turbines, the power plant generates about 1.8 million **kilowatts** of electricity for both countries.

Industry and the Environment

Offering cheap power and a convenient transportation route, the St. Lawrence River has attracted many industrial plants, ranging from grain elevators to cement factories, to its shores. However, the growth of industry has also greatly affected the St. Lawrence basin's environment.

Some industries along the St. Lawrence River and the Great Lakes have polluted the river by dumping **PCBs** and other chemicals that are harmful to animals and humans. PCBs are environmental pollutants that build up in animal tissues. They are linked to the development of cancer and other diseases in humans and animals. **Pesticides** and fertilizers used in agriculture along the St. Lawrence River seep into the **groundwater** and drain into the river.

The construction of the St. Lawrence Seaway contributed to pollution of the river as well. **Dredging** to deepen and widen channels so that they could accommodate larger ships stirred up contaminants that had been sitting on the bottom of the river.

Invasive Species

Another ecological threat to the river is the introduction of nonnative, or **invasive**, species of fish and plant life. These plants or animals are not naturally found in the St. Lawrence River; they have been introduced, often in the **ballast** water of foreign ships that traveled through the seaway. The ballast water may have been added to a ship at its point of origin to add weight and stability, then pumped out of the ship at its destination in the St. Lawrence–Great Lakes system.

Invasive species can threaten native species by preying on them or by outcompeting them for food.

Road to Recovery

Governments and organizations have taken action in response to threats to the St. Lawrence River. Thanks to environmental preservation efforts that began in the late 1970s, the St. Lawrence River is now one of the cleanest rivers in the world. Over the past three decades, the governments of Canada and the United States have funded large-scale cleanup and pollution prevention programs in the St. Lawrence River–Great Lakes system. Many concerned citizens also work with private organizations to help clean up the river's waters and protect river life.

Mussel Invasion

Zebra mussels arrived in the St. Lawrence Seaway in 1986 in the ballast water of a ship from across the Atlantic Ocean. Since then, zebra mussels have spread throughout the St. Lawrence River and the Great Lakes. This small but destructive freshwater mussel can grow to be two inches (five centimeters) in size. Zebra mussels consume algae, the main food for many native species in the St. Lawrence River.

The zebra mussel is an invasive species in the St. Lawrence River-Great Lakes system.

COMPARING THE WORLD'S RIVERS

River	Continent	Source	Outflow	Approximate Length in miles (kilometers)	Area of Drainage Basin in square miles (square kilometers)
Amazon	South America	Andes Mountains, Peru	Atlantic Ocean	4,000 (6,450)	2.7 million (7 million)
Euphrates	Asia	Murat and Kara Su rivers, Turkey	Persian Gulf	1,740 (2,800)	171,430 (444,000)
Ganges	Asia	Himalayas, India	Bay of Bengal	1,560 (2,510)	400,000 (1 million)
Mississippi	North America	Lake Itasca, Minnesota	Gulf of Mexico	2,350 (3,780)	1.2 million (3.1 million)
Nile	Africa	Streams flowing into Lake Victoria, East Africa	Mediterranean Sea	4,145 (6,670)	1.3 million (3.3 million)
Rhine	Europe	Alps, Switzerland	North Sea	865 (1,390)	65,600 (170,000)
St. Lawrence	North America	Lake Ontario, Canada and United States	Gulf of St. Lawrence	744 (1,190)	502,000 (1.3 million)
Tigris	Asia	Lake Hazar, Taurus Mountains, Turkey	Persian Gulf	1,180 (1,900)	43,000 (111,000)
Yangtze	Asia	Damqu River, Tanggula Mountains, China	East China Sea	3,915 (6,300)	690,000 (1.8 million)

TIMELINE

12,000 years ago	Water from melting glaciers begins to fill the Great Lakes and form the Champlain Sea in the St. Lawrence region.
10,000 years ago	Indigenous people are living in eastern Canada.
6,000–6,500 years ago	After an uplift of the land causes most of the Champlain Sea to drain into the Atlantic, the St. Lawrence River flows in its present-day course.
1497	Italian explorer John Cabot sails to Canada. He reaches the east coast near Newfoundland and claims the area for England.
1534	French explorer Jacques Cartier sails into the Gulf of St. Lawrence.
1535	Cartier returns to North America and sails up the St. Lawrence River.
1608	Samuel de Champlain starts a French colony at the site of modern-day Quebec City.
1754–1763	Britain defeats France in the French and Indian War. The land in North America granted to the British under the treaty ending the war includes most of the land surrounding the St. Lawrence River.
1825	The Lachine Canal opens, allowing ships to travel farther up the St. Lawrence River into the interior of North America from the Atlantic Ocean.
1829	The first Welland Canal opens, bypassing Niagara Falls and enabling ships to travel between Lake Ontario and Lake Erie.
1959	The St. Lawrence Seaway officially opens on June 26.
2009	The St. Lawrence Seaway celebrates its 50th anniversary as a vital transportation route between the Atlantic and central North America.

GLOSSARY

allied Joined or united in a close relationship

ballast Heavy material that is placed in the hold of a ship to enhance stability

bilingual Using or able to use two languages (such as English and French)

canals Human-made waterways that are used for shipping and irrigation

commodities Economic goods, such as farm crops or mined materials

crater A bowl-shaped depression or hole

dendritic Branching like a tree

drainage basin The area of land drained by a river and its tributaries

drainage pattern The arrangement of a main stream and its tributaries

dredging Deepening (as a waterway) with a digging machine

ecology The relationship between living and nonliving things and the environment in which they exist

economic Relating to the way money and goods are produced, consumed, and distributed

estuary A large, tidal mouth of a river where freshwater mixes with saltwater from the ocean the river is approaching

extinction Having died out completely

fluvial Relating to or inhabiting a river or stream

glacier Large body of ice and snow moving slowly down a slope or spreading outward on land

groundwater Water within Earth, especially that supplies wells and springs

habitat The environment in which a certain plant or animal naturally lives and grows

hydroelectricity Electricity produced by using the movement of water

indigenous Originating, living, or occurring naturally in a particular region or environment

invasive Having the tendency to spread

kilowatt A unit of electrical power

locks Human-made structures in a waterway that allow boats to be raised and lowered

migration Periodic movement from one region to another for feeding or breeding

mouth The place where a river enters a larger body of water

PCBs Environmental pollutants that build up in animal tissue and can cause health problems (PCB stands for polychlorinated biphenyl)

pesticides Chemicals used to kill insects and other pests that harm crops or other plants

reservoirs Artificial lakes where water is collected and kept for use

trellis An arrangement that looks like a framework of crossed strips

tributaries Streams that flow into a larger stream or other body of water

turbines Machines that produce a turning action (for example, when their blades are pushed by moving water); turbines are often connected to generators to produce electricity

valves Devices that regulate the flow of gases or liquids by opening, closing, or blocking passageways

FIND OUT MORE

BOOKS

Daigle, Evelyne. *As Long as There Are Whales*. Tundra Books, 2004.

Foran, Jill. *The Great Lakes*. Weigl Publishers, 2008.

Kalman, Bobbie. *Nations of the Eastern Great Lakes*. Crabtree Publishing Company, 2004.

Kummer, Patricia K. *The Great Lakes*. Marshall Cavendish, 2008.

Lackey, Jennifer. *Jacques Cartier: Exploring the St. Lawrence River*. Crabtree Publishing Company, 2007.

McNeese, Tim. *The St. Lawrence River*. Chelsea House, 2005.

WEB SITES

Great Canadian Rivers: The St. Lawrence River
www.greatcanadianrivers.com/rivers/stlawer/stlawer-home.html

Great Lakes Kids
www.on.ec.gc.ca/greatlakes/For_Kids-WS4DB7BBAD-1_En.htm

St. Lawrence Centre
www.qc.ec.gc.ca/csl

St. Lawrence Seaway
www.greatlakes-seaway.com

ABOUT THE AUTHOR

Lynn Peppas is a writer of children's nonfiction books. She has always been a bookworm and grew up reading all the books she could. She feels fortunate to have been able to combine her love of reading and her love of kids into a career. Her work in children's publishing is a dream-job come true.

INDEX

Page references in **bold** type are to illustrations.